Thank You, Friend

COLLEEN L. REECE
and
JULIE REECE-DEMARCO

DayMaker
GREETING BOOKS

Thank You, Friend

There is a special comfort that comes from knowing we will never have to face anything alone in this life. Friends will always be there to rejoice with us in our joys and support us through our greatest sorrows. Few things on this earth have more power to heal heartache, conquer loneliness, create happiness, or foster love, than friendship. It is one of God's most precious gifts to His children. He asks us to share that gift with others.

Beloved, let us love one another:
for love is of God;
and every one that loveth is born of God,
and knoweth God.

1 JOHN 4:7 KJV

Thank you for being my friend.

The Most Excellent Way

And now I will show you the most excellent way.
If I speak in the tongues of men and of angels, but
have not love, I am only a resounding gong
or a clanging cymbal.
If I have the gift of prophecy and can fathom all mysteries
and all knowledge, and if I have a faith that can move
mountains, but have not love, I am nothing.
If I give all I possess to the poor and surrender my
body to the flames, but have not love, I gain nothing.
Love is patient, love is kind. It does not envy,
it does not boast, it is not proud.
It is not rude, it is not self-seeking, it is not
easily angered, it keeps no record of wrongs.
Love does not delight in evil but rejoices with the truth. It
always protects, always trusts, always hopes, always perseveres.

*Love never fails. But where there are prophecies,
they will cease; where there are tongues, they will be
stilled; where there is knowledge, it will pass away.*

*For we know in part and we prophesy in part,
but when perfection comes, the imperfect disappears.*

*When I was a child, I talked like a child, I thought like a
child, I reasoned like a child. When I became a man, I put childish
ways behind me.*

*Now we see but a poor reflection as in a mirror; then we shall
see face to face. Now I know in part; then I shall know fully,
even as I am fully known.*

*And now these three remain: faith, hope and love. But the
greatest of these is love.*

1 CORINTHIANS 12:31–13:13 NIV

Thank you for loving me.

Who Is My Friend?

Webster defines the word "neighborly" as also being "friendly." Luke 10:27 indicates Jesus may have felt the same. When asked what one must do to inherit eternal life, He replied, "What is written in the law?"

"Thou shalt love the Lord thy God with all thy heart, and with all thy soul, and with all thy strength, and with all thy mind; and thy neighbour as thyself," the attorney promptly quoted.

"Thou hast answered right: this do and thou shalt live," Jesus promised. The lawyer wasn't satisfied.

Jesus then told one of the most quoted stories in the New Testament: the parable of the Good Samaritan.

A certain man went down from Jerusalem to Jericho, on a stretch of highway notorious for attacks on travelers by bands of roving outlaws. Robbers fell on the man, stripped him of his clothing, beat him, and left him to die beside the road.

A priest, going the same way, saw the victim but didn't stop to help. Perhaps he was late for an appointment. Perhaps he didn't wish to be made unclean. In any event, he "passed by on the other side" of the road. So did a Levite—a lesser ceremonial officer.

Then came a Samaritan, whose people were sworn enemies of the Jews. He saw the man lying senseless beside the road. Unlike the two who had passed by earlier, pity and compassion spawned action.

He knelt in the dusty road, poured oil and wine on the victim's wounds, and bandaged them. He put the unfortunate traveler on his own donkey, took him to an inn, and to the amazement of the innkeeper, continued to minister to him.

The next day, the Samaritan handed the disbelieving innkeeper some money. He told him to take care of the injured man, and that when he returned, he would pay for whatever expenses had been incurred on the man's behalf.

Jesus concluded his story by asking the lawyer, "Which of these three do you think was a neighbor to the man who fell into the hands of robbers?"

· · ·

The nameless traveler in Jesus' story has been admired throughout history as a shining example of one who cares.

Thank you, friend,
for showing what a true neighbor really is.

The Tenth Leper

I f I could be anyone in history who would I be?" I listened attentively as Dave,* a young father twisted from a painful, ongoing battle with multiple sclerosis, posed the question. Who would he choose? Certainly someone of good health. A person who had lived strong and free from pain. Glancing at his young children and pretty wife, I knew it would be someone who had counted many birthdays. Who had treasured the opportunity to see his family grow. Who had bounced grandchildren on his knee and kissed his wife of many years before retiring to bed.

I recalled the beautiful, detailed drawings lining the walls of his home, marked with Dave's signature. They evidenced his talent before the ravages of this disease robbed his hands of their precision. Perhaps a great artist would be his choice?

Dave cleared his throat and announced, "After a lot of thought I decided—I would be the tenth leper."

His answer floored me. The tenth leper? A man who lived a

---

* symbol indicates name has been changed

good portion of his life in the bonds of a terrible illness. Ostracized. Shunned. How could Dave, so familiar with pain himself, choose this path? His answer humbled me.

"You see, the tenth leper recognized the great gift the Savior had given him. He was able to look Christ in the eyes and personally thank Him for His wonderful blessings. He could grasp His hand and express his gratitude. If I could do anything in history, I would choose the opportunity to look my Savior in the eyes and thank Him for *my* many blessings."

. . .

Dave's answer stayed with me over the weeks to come. For how many of my blessings had I failed to thank the Lord? How many had I failed to even recognize were blessings?

We don't know much about the other nine lepers. Perhaps some were overwhelmed with joy and ran to reacquaint themselves with loving family members. Maybe they returned to tell other friends and fellow lepers in the colony the glorious news of their healing. We do not know what they did do. But we know what they did *not* do—they failed to express their gratitude to the Giver of their gift. Since listening to Dave, I have tried to be more conscious of my blessings—and where they come from. Although I can't currently take my Savior's hand and express my gratitude like the tenth leper, I can take the hands of my friends and acquaintances and relay my thanks.

Thank you for
the blessings you bring to my life.

*"I will not follow where the path may lead,
but I will go where there is no path,
and I will leave a trail."*

MURIEL STRODE

"True friends walk close beside you in the shade,
not just in the sunshine."

ANONYMOUS

Thank you for always being there
when I need you.

. . .

"Those who bring sunshine to the lives of others
cannot keep it from themselves."

SIR JAMES MATTHEW BARRIE

Thank you for the sunshine
you bring into my life.

Touching Shoulders

There's a comforting thought at the
    close of the day,
When I'm weary and lonely and sad,
That sort of grips hold of my crusty old heart
And bids it be merry and glad.

It gets in my soul and it drives out the blues,
And finally thrills, through and through.
It is just a sweet memory that chants the refrain:
"I'm glad I touch shoulders with you!"

Did you know you were brave, did you know
    you were strong?
Did you know there was one leaning hard?
Did you know that I waited and listened and
    prayed,
And was cheered by your simplest word?

Thank You, Friend

Did you know that I longed for that smile on
    your face,
For the sound of your voice ringing true?
Did you know I grew stronger and better because
I had merely touched shoulders with you?

I am glad that I live, that I battle and strive
For the place that I know I must fill;
I am thankful for sorrows, I'll meet with a grin
What fortune may send, good or ill.

I may not have wealth, I may not be great,
But I know I shall always be true,
For I have in my life that courage you gave
When once I rubbed shoulders with you.

AUTHOR UNKNOWN

Thank you, friend,
for inspiring me to live up to my potential.

*"How far that little candle throws his beams!
So shines a good deed in a naughty world."*

WILLIAM SHAKESPEARE

When Three's Not a Crowd

It started with a seemingly inconsequential good deed. Fourteen-year-old Connie had won a role in the play, "Little Women," but had a problem. Living four miles out of town in the days when few students had cars posed transportation difficulties. Play practice right after school wasn't so bad—her dad could come get her after his long, hard day of work. Evening practices created a greater problem. Connie's father had to get up before dawn cracked, which meant early bedtime. He needed to be asleep long before practice ended. Should she turn down the part, even though being chosen was an honor?

After hearing Connie's dilemma, Josey, a fellow sophomore, promptly offered, "You can stay with me on the nights we have late practice."

Her kindness was the beginning of a lasting, lifelong friendship between Connie, Josey, and her twin sister Joanne. They became inseparable from that first sleepover. All through high school, marriage, children, and careers, their early friendship—sparked by the simple, kind deed—has shone bright and unwavering.

Connie has been blessed with many wonderful friends since the days of "Little Women." None will ever take the twins' place. Neither distance nor busy schedules affect the bond between them. When the three do get together, they simply pick up where they left off.

Thank you
for enriching my life with your caring.

The Secret

"What is the secret of your life?" Mrs. Elizabeth Barrett Browning, the poet, once asked novelist Charles Kingsley. "Tell me, that I may make mine beautiful also." The well-loved author thought for a moment, then quietly said, "I had a friend."

Thank you
for helping me make my life beautiful.

If I Can Stop One Heart From Breaking

If I can stop one heart from breaking,
    I shall not live in vain;
If I can ease one life the aching,
    Or cool one pain,
Or help one lonely person
    Into happiness again
I shall not live in vain.

EMILY DICKINSON

I am grateful your life has touched mine.

Being There

Real friends do not batter down doors or force
their way into our lives. They knock, then
patiently wait for us to unlock our innermost
feelings and invite them to enter and share.

Except for a year away from home to attend business
college, I either lived at home or had Mom living with me.
We shared fifty-six years of companionship, including more
than two decades between the time Dad passed on in 1968
and Mom left me in 1992, at age ninety-five. The day she
died, I lost a mother, best friend, editor, proofreader—
and my staunchest supporter.

The faith inherited from generations past helped sustain
me, but it couldn't fill Mom's empty chair or the hole in
my heart. Yet in the months that followed, my standard
answer to "How are you doing?" was always "Fine."
About six months after Mom died, my dear friend and
minister's wife, Betty, asked her usual Sunday morning
question, "How are you doing?"

"Fine," I said, launching into a recitation of the new writing projects God had provided to keep me busy.

She quietly listened. When I ran out of words she looked deep into my eyes and asked, "How are you *really* doing?"

Her gentle repetition shattered the wall I'd unknowingly built between me and those who could have helped so much more than I had allowed them to. "I'm falling apart inside," I told her.

My response opened the door for me to pour out the depths of pain and loneliness I'd refrained from sharing. It also opened the door to the beginning of healing.

Thank you, friend,
for knowing when to knock. . .
and when to knock a second time.

The Arrow and the Song

I shot an arrow into the air,
It fell to earth, I knew not where;
For, so swiftly it flew, the sight
Could not follow it in its flight.

I breathed a song into the air,
It fell to earth, I knew not where;
For who has sight so keen and strong,
That it can follow the flight of song?

Long, long afterward, in an oak
I found the arrow, still unbroke;
And the song, from beginning to end,
I found again in the heart of a friend.

HENRY WADSWORTH LONGFELLOW

Thank you
for the song you carry in your heart.

"We do not wish for friends

to feed and clothe our bodies—

neighbors are kind enough for that—

but to do the like office for our spirits."

HENRY DAVID THOREAU

Take Two Cookies and Call Me in the Morning

*Jesus. . .saith unto him, "Go home to thy friends,
and tell them how great things the Lord hath done for thee,
and hath had compassion on thee."*

MARK 5:19 KJV

Janea stared at the unfamiliar name on the piece of paper. As part of a program to ensure no one fell through the cracks, her church group had assigned each college student someone to "watch over" for the new school year. Janea and her roommate, Sarah, got Lacey. The problem was, Janea wasn't sure why. Lacey, a single, pregnant, seventeen-year-old girl, five hundred miles from home, needed far more support and wisdom than either Janea or Sarah had to give.

"There must be a mistake," the roommates determined that evening. They vowed to talk to the pastor on Sunday, sure that once he was fully aware of the situation, they'd be given another assignment.

They were wrong. The pastor's gentle smile and firm head shake spoke volumes. "I'm not sure *why* God wanted you two to have Lacey, but He did. I'm sure you will do a wonderful job."

The girls did not share Pastor Anderson's confidence. Month after month they attempted to visit and befriend Lacey, but could not rid themselves of the feelings of inadequacy. While their biggest worries were tests and which boys they would date on Friday night, Lacey struggled with whether to keep her baby or give it up for adoption.

Unable to provide counsel or advice, the girls did the only things they could—visited once or twice a month, and periodically dropped treats and goodies by the doorstep of Lacey's apartment. "As good as your chocolate chip cookies are," Janea confided in Sarah one evening, "Lacey's got problems even they can't touch. She really needs someone with experience and wisdom—*not us.*"

Their feelings of inadequacy grew when the call from the hospital came. "Lacey is in labor. The adoptive couple is already here. She asked if you'd come."

Sarah and Janea headed for the hospital at a loss for words of comfort to offer. Neither had attended a birth before, much less supported a mother trying to give a child to another couple. And they weren't even sure Lacey *liked* them.

When they arrived, Lacey's mom met them at the door. "My plane just touched down. You must be Janea and Sarah."

The girls looked at each other perplexedly. How did Lacey's mom know who they were?

The answer was quick in coming.

Tears filled the woman's eyes as she took the girls' hands in her own. "I can never tell you how thankful I am for what you've done for Lacey. You don't know how many times she came home after a particularly hard day and found one of your treats on her porch. She said she never could have made it through this time without you. You were heaven-sent."

The girls stepped into Lacey's room as the girl handed her son over to the young adoptive couple. Despite the tears glistening in Lacey's eyes, Sarah and Janea were, for once, not at a loss for words.

They headed to the bedside, gave Lacey a hug, and placed flowers next to her bed. The two had just learned a valuable lesson. Sometimes chocolate chip cookies and a visit can speak louder than even the most profound words.

Thank you
for showing me love and friendship
through your kind actions.

Thank You, Friend

It is in loving, not in being loved,
The heart finds its quest;
It is in giving, not in getting,
Our lives are blest.

AUTHOR UNKNOWN

Thank you
for blessing others with your love.

A Friend in Deed

"A friend in need is a friend indeed."
MEDIEVAL PROVERB

From childhood, Susan* admired her grandmother's ring. Not for its monetary value, but because the precious jewels sparkled with every change of light. Before Susan's grandmother died, she gave the ring to her childless daughter, Abigail.* "Someday it will be yours," Abigail promised Susan.

Years later, Abigail passed on. When her will was read, Susan discovered she had evidently forgotten her promise. She bequeathed the ring to someone outside the family. Susan was shocked and disappointed. Then a message came.

Even though the ring was left to me, I don't feel it is mine. I've always known where your grandmother and Abigail intended it to go. As soon as I receive it, I will give it to its rightful owner—you.

It was signed by the person who had inherited the valuable piece of jewelry.

Thank you for being a friend of deeds.

29

Words to Live By

*"True friends are those who are better together
than either of them could be alone."*

ANONYMOUS

. . .

"Hold a true friend with both your hands."

NIGERIAN PROVERB

. . .

*"A friend is someone who knows the song in your heart
and can sing it back to you when
you have forgotten the words."*

AUTHOR UNKNOWN

"Friendship is
one mind in two bodies."

MENCIUS

. . .

"The only way to have a friend is to be one."

RALPH WALDO EMERSON

Shining

A little child stood in a great cathedral on a
summer day. Sunlight streamed through the
beautiful stained glass windows, making the figures
etched on them brilliant with color.
Later, someone asked, "What is a saint?"
The child immediately replied, "Someone who
lets the light shine through."

ANONYMOUS

Friends also let the light shine through.
Thank you.

"A friend is one who incessantly pays us
the compliment of expecting from us all the virtues,
and who can appreciate them in us."

HENRY DAVID THOREAU

Thank you
for encouraging me to become my best.

Saving Sympathy

Following the death of an elderly woman, a multitude of friends and acquaintances offered condolences to her companion of many years. Neighbors brought in food. Telephone calls helped fill the rooms that had once rung with conversation. Yet, after a time, even the most loving friends went back to their own lives and contented themselves with sporadic and increasingly less frequent acts of kindness. Then Meredith* stepped in, doing what she had promised mutual friends at the funeral.

"Right now, everyone is giving needed support," she had told them. "Flowers, cards, time. . . I am going to hold off, wait and watch for the next few months. There will be times when Robert* will need love and comfort. He may not be willing or able to express how much he is hurting, or how much he needs a listening ear."

She smiled. "I will save my flowers, my cards—and, most of all, my time—for then."

Thank you for recognizing when
I most need evidence of your friendship.

A *friend loveth at all times.*

PROVERBS 17:17 KJV

. . .

"Friendship is always
a sweet responsibility,
never an opportunity."

KAHLIL GIBRAN

May Day

Riley Collins's day started like any other—badly.
Up at 5 A.M., in the shower, bagel on the go,
and off to another day of corporate drudgery.
Only this morning, as she wearily opened her front
door, she nearly stumbled across a bouquet of fresh tulips.
"What on earth?" Riley's face twisted in surprise. No one
ever brought her flowers. At least not since she and her
boyfriend had called it quits in an ugly break-up six months
before. The attached card added to her bewilderment. Simple
block letters spelled her name and the message: *Thinking of you.*
Have a nice May Day. The author remained anonymous.
Despite her hectic work schedule, Riley's mind wandered.
Who would have left the gift? Her suppositions continued at
home. Gazing at the flowers adorning her once-barren table,
she smiled. *Well, whoever it was sure brightened my day.*
The next morning she awakened, glanced at the tulips, and
smiled again. Opening the door, she was amazed to find another
pot of flowers. This time purple hyacinths poked from the con-
tainer—but the card read the same: *Have a nice May Day.*

Day after day the pattern continued—fresh flowers and a note. Each morning Riley became progressively more excited to begin her day. Soon the trip to check the front door was made before dressing, showering, or eating.

June first arrived. Riley opened the door, but there weren't any flowers. Disappointment reigned until she turned and faced her front room, now filled to capacity with blooms. The smile that had frequented her face so often the past month returned to its rightful place. She quickly dressed and headed out the door.

At the local flower shop Riley picked out a pot of tulips and a small card. She almost skipped on her way to Mrs. Landry's house. Riley glanced at the yellow ribbon that would remain hung until the Landry's son safely returned from military service abroad and carefully placed the flowers. The anonymous note read: *Have a nice June Day.*

Thank you for brightening all of my days.

Greater love hath no man than this,
that a man lay down his life for his friends.

JOHN 15:13 KJV

The Simple Things

I watched the airplanes fly their course into the two
    great towers.
The seconds crept by endlessly. The silence seemed like hours.

I clutched my heart in disbelief, my head I bowed with shame
To see such devastation wrought in Deity's Great Name.

Then through the ashes, clouds of dust, and crumbling
    steel, emerged
The engines bright; heroic souls upon the place converged.

I saw fine men, with families, who bravely faced the fire,
And vowed their sacrificial acts, my own life would inspire.

Thank You, Friend

I heard the calls to cherished ones, good-byes filled with love
And kissed my own dear ones to sleep and
    thanked the Lord above.

Images of sleepless friends, who searched both
    night and day
Reminded me of my own friends and things I *had* to say.

The Stars and Stripes that draped the hole, and marked the
    sacred spot
Renewed my prayer not to forget my freedoms were hard fought.

So on that day of misery—of grief and terror and strife
I learned the simple things we have are worth the most in life.

And on that day, I took a vow. I would not go to bed
With angry heart. . .or jealous thoughts. . .
    or thank yous left unsaid.

JULIE REECE-DEMARCO

Thank you for all of the gifts and laughter
you have brought into my life.

"So long as we love, we serve.
So long as we are loved by others,
I would almost say we are indispensable;
and no man is useless while he has a friend."

ROBERT LOUIS STEVENSON

Thank You, Friend.